Frugal Livii
Beginners (

Learn 100 Creative Ways to Cut Expenses, Save Money and Live Stress Free

Table of Contents

Introduction

Chapter 1: Introduction to Frugal Living

Chapter 2: Setting the Foundation to Frugal Living

Chapter 3: 100 Creative Ways to Cut Expenses

Chapter 4: DIY Frugality

Chapter 5: Frugal Living Beyond the Basics

Chapter 6: Stress-Free Frugal Living

Chapter 7: Frugal Family Living

Chapter 8: Sustaining Frugal Living Practices

Conclusion

Introduction

Hey there! If you're anything like me, the hustle and bustle of daily life can feel like a never-ending marathon, always trying to keep up with the latest trends. But what if I told you there's another way? What if I could cut through the noise, save some cash, and live a life with a lot less stress? Welcome to my guide on frugal living, where I'm sharing my journey and the lessons I've learned for anyone looking to shake up their finances and discover a simpler, intentional way of life.

So, here's the deal. We're going to unravel the layers of frugal living together, starting with the basics. Let's break down what it really means to live frugally, not as a sacrifice, but as a powerful choice that can transform how I view money and happiness.

Once I've got that frugal mindset locked in, I'll move on to building a solid financial base. No complicated jargon or overwhelming spreadsheets here – just practical steps to assess my finances and create a budget that actually works for me.

Now, here's where it gets exciting. I'm handing myself a playbook of 100 creative and doable ways to cut my expenses. From grocery hacks that won't have me eating rice and beans every day to clever strategies to lower my utility bills, I'm arming myself with the tools to make a real impact on my wallet.

But it's not all about penny-pinching. I'm a big fan of rolling up my sleeves and getting hands-on. DIY frugality is my next stop, where I'll explore the satisfaction of fixing things around the house and repurposing items in a way that not only saves money but adds a dash of creativity to my life.

As I journey through this, I'll also touch on advanced strategies, stress-free living principles, and ways to make frugality a family affair. It's not just about cutting back; it's about finding a balanced and sustainable way for me to live that sets me on a path to financial stability and genuine contentment.

So, buckle up and get ready to explore the transformative world of frugal living with me. It's not about giving up the good stuff; it's about redefining what the good stuff really is. Let's dive in and discover how a simpler, intentional life might just be the key to my financial freedom and stress-free living.

Chapter 1- Introduction to Frugal Living

Picture this: a regular person, just like you and me, buried under a mountain of bills, grappling with the relentless whirlwind of financial pressures, and yearning for a way out. That person is me, and I'm here to share my journey into the realm of frugal living – a journey fueled by the desire for financial sanity, intentional choices, and a life that's not dictated by the constant chase for more.

Discovering Frugal Living:

Let's start at the beginning. The term "frugal living" had always sounded a bit, well, boring to me. But then I began to realize it's not about deprivation or living like a hermit; it's about recalibrating how I interact with money. It's about making choices that align with my values, cutting out the excess, and embracing a more intentional way of living. So, armed with curiosity and a tinge of skepticism, I decided to dive into this world headfirst.

Making Every Dollar Count:

Now, let's talk about money – that elusive thing that seems to slip through our fingers like sand. The realization hit me like a ton of bricks: I needed to be smarter with my cash. No more mindless spending, no more impulse buys. Instead, I'm on a mission to make every single dollar count. Whether it's a cup of coffee or a new gadget, I'm asking myself, "Does this truly add value to my life?" It's about decluttering not just my physical space but also my financial space.

Shifting My Money Mindset:

Frugal living isn't about becoming a modern-day Ebenezer Scrooge, hoarding pennies and scowling at joy. It's a mindset shift, a conscious rebellion against the societal pressure to keep up with the ever-changing trends. It's about redefining what success looks like and choosing experiences over possessions. This chapter is about freeing myself from the mental shackles of consumerism and realizing that, hey, I make the rules here.

Taking Control of My Finances:

Enter the realm of financial liberation. Imagine feeling like your money is a partner in this journey, not a relentless dictator. Frugal living is my strategy for taking back control, for turning my money into a tool that works for me, not against me. It's about building a safety net for the unexpected twists and turns life throws my way, and finally having a say in where my hard-earned money goes.

So, here's the deal: this journey into frugal living isn't just a series of financial tweaks. It's a profound reevaluation of my relationship with money, a chance to rewrite my money story, and a quest for a life that's both satisfying and sensible. If you're up for a ride that goes beyond budget sheets and enters the territory of profound financial and personal transformation, then buckle up. Join me as we navigate the complex waters of frugal living, make savvy choices, and embark on an adventure that promises to redefine our relationship with money and, ultimately, our lives.

Chapter 2- Setting the Foundation to Frugal Living

Alright, let's pull out the magnifying glass because we're about to zoom into the intricate details of setting the foundation for my frugal living journey. It's not just about squeezing pennies; it's about constructing a fortress of financial resilience that can weather any storm life throws my way while allowing me to flourish. So, buckle up as I delve into the nitty-gritty of this blueprint for financial strength.

Assessing My Finances: A Deep Dive into the Money Waters

Imagine this as a financial excavation, where I'm donning my explorer hat and plunging into the often murky waters of my finances. I'm laying out all my cards on the table, staring at the numbers, and asking the tough questions. What's my income? What are my fixed expenses? Where is my money disappearing like a magician's disappearing act?

I'm not just looking for problems; I'm seeking insights. This deep dive is about discovering where my money is already working for me, identifying areas of potential improvement, and acknowledging both wins and oops moments.

Creating a Frugal Budget: More Than Just Numbers on a Page

Now, let's talk budgets. I used to dread this part, but not anymore. It's not about turning into a budgeting automaton; it's about creating a dynamic tool that reflects the ebb and flow of my life. Every dollar gets a purpose, a role to play in the grand financial narrative.

Rent or mortgage? Groceries? Savings? Entertainment? They all have a place in this budget. It's not about restriction; it's about taking control. This budget isn't just numbers on a page; it's a financial GPS guiding me toward my goals.

Emergency Fund: My Financial Safety Net

Picture this as my financial safety net – the emergency fund. It's the unsung hero that swoops in when life decides to throw a curveball. Whether it's a medical emergency, car trouble, or a global pandemic, having an emergency fund means I'm not clutching at straws when the waters get rough.

I'm setting a realistic goal, understanding that Rome wasn't built in a day. Three to six months' worth of living expenses is the target, but I'm starting where I can and gradually building it up. It's my insurance against life's unexpected twists.

Debt Tackling Strategy: Breaking Free, Step by Step

Debt – that four-letter word that can feel like an anchor. It's time to face it head-on. I'm evaluating my debts, whether it's credit cards, student loans, or other financial obligations. This isn't about drowning in guilt; it's about creating a strategy to tackle it.

I'll prioritize high-interest debts first, systematically paying them off like a ninja targeting the biggest threats. As each debt gets crossed off the list, I'm redirecting that money towards the next one in line. It's a slow and steady march towards financial freedom.

Savings Goals: Dreaming Big While Staying Practical

Now, let's talk dreams. Big dreams, small dreams, and everything in between. I'm setting savings goals that align with my aspirations, whether it's a vacation, a new gadget, or building a nest egg for the future. Each goal is a stepping stone toward financial success.

I'm not just throwing numbers into the void; I'm attaching emotions to these goals. Visualizing the reward of my efforts keeps me motivated. It's not just about the destination; it's about enjoying the journey, one frugally earned dollar at a time.

Insurance: Shielding My Finances from Life's Curveballs

Insurance – the unsung hero of financial planning. It's my shield against the unexpected. Whether it's health insurance, car insurance, or other forms of protection, I'm ensuring that my finances have a safety net. After all, I'd rather have insurance and not need it than need it and not have it.

Education and Continuous Learning: Sharpening My Financial Savvy

Knowledge is power, especially in the world of finance. I'm committing to ongoing financial education. Whether it's books, podcasts, or online courses, I'm staying informed about personal finance strategies, investment opportunities, and frugal living hacks. The more I know, the more confidently I can navigate the financial landscape.

So, there you have it – the intricacies of how I'm laying the groundwork for my frugal living journey. It's not just about tightening the purse strings; it's about crafting a comprehensive blueprint for financial resilience, where every decision contributes to the fortress of my financial well-being. Stay tuned as we go even deeper into the world of intentional and savvy frugal living.

Chapter 3- 100 Creative Ways to Cut Expenses

Alright, grab a notepad because we're about to embark on a journey through the vast landscape of creative expense-cutting. This chapter isn't just about saving a few bucks; it's a comprehensive guide to mastering the art of frugality. Buckle up as we explore 100 detailed and creative ways to trim the fat from my expenses and boost my financial well-being.

Grocery Shopping Hacks: Mastering the Supermarket Game

Meal Planning Magic: Before stepping foot in the grocery store, I'm planning my meals for the week. It reduces impulse buys and ensures I only purchase what I need.

Embrace Generic Brands: Let go of brand loyalty and embrace generic or store-brand products. They often offer the same quality at a lower cost.

Bulk Buying Brilliance: Purchasing non-perishables in bulk can significantly reduce the per-unit cost. Think rice, pasta, and canned goods.

Reducing Utility Bills: Energy-Efficient Living

Smart Thermostats: Investing in a smart thermostat helps optimize heating and cooling, saving energy and money in the long run.

Unplug and Save: Devices on standby mode still consume energy. Unplugging electronics when not in use can lead to noticeable savings on the electricity bill.

LED Lighting Upgrade: Switching to energy-efficient LED bulbs is an upfront cost that pays off over time with lower energy consumption and longer lifespan.

Thrifty Transportation: Moving Around on a Budget

Carpooling Communities: Joining carpooling communities or coordinating rides with colleagues can significantly cut down on fuel expenses.

Public Transportation Perks: Where possible, opt for public transportation. Monthly passes or bulk ticket purchases often come with discounts.

Embrace Biking: If feasible, consider biking for short-distance commuting. It's not only cost-effective but also a healthy choice.

DIY Maintenance: Fixing and Upgrading Without Breaking the Bank

Learn Basic Home Repairs: YouTube is a treasure trove of DIY home repair tutorials. From fixing leaks to repairing minor electrical issues, learning the basics can save on handyman costs.

Upcycling Furniture: Instead of splurging on new furniture, I'm exploring the world of upcycling. A fresh coat of paint or some creative tweaks can breathe new life into old pieces.

Gardening Greenery: Growing my own herbs and vegetables not only provides fresh produce but also trims the grocery bill. A win-win for the wallet and the palate.

Frugal Fashion: Stylish on a Shoestring Budget

Thrift Shop Treasures: Thrift shopping is a goldmine for stylish finds at a fraction of the cost. It's sustainable and easy on the wallet.

Clothing Swaps: Hosting or participating in clothing swaps with friends can bring a fresh wardrobe without spending a dime.

DIY Clothing Repairs: Basic sewing skills can save me from replacing a garment every time a button pops off or a seam unravels.

Entertainment and Leisure: Having Fun Without Draining the Wallet

Library Love: Libraries offer a vast array of books, movies, and even audiobooks for free. It's an entertainment treasure trove waiting to be explored.

Free Events and Activities: Many communities host free events, from outdoor concerts to art festivals. It's a chance to have a good time without spending a dime.

DIY Hobbies: Instead of pricey hobbies, I'm exploring DIY alternatives. From painting to crafting, it's a creative outlet that doesn't break the bank.

Digital Deals: Navigating the Online World of Savings

Cashback Apps: Utilizing cashback apps for everyday purchases adds up over time. It's like getting a discount every time I shop.

Online Coupon Platforms: Before making any online purchase, I'm checking coupon platforms for potential discounts. It takes a few minutes and can result in significant savings.

Free Software Alternatives: Many paid software programs have free alternatives with similar features. It's about finding quality without the hefty price tag.

Financial Organization: Streamlining Money Matters

Automate Savings: Setting up automatic transfers to a savings account ensures I'm consistently putting money away, even if it's a small amount.

Negotiate Bills: A simple phone call to service providers can lead to discounts or better deals. It's a negotiation game that's often overlooked.

Review Subscriptions: Periodically reviewing subscription services helps identify ones that are no longer essential. Canceling or downgrading can free up funds.

Mindful Eating: Savvy Choices in the Kitchen

Cook in Batches: Cooking in batches and freezing portions not only saves time but also curbs the temptation to order takeout on busy nights.

Leftover Remix: Get creative with leftovers. A bit of innovation can turn last night's dinner into a whole new culinary experience.

Limit Dining Out: While dining out is a treat, limiting it to special occasions can make it more enjoyable and budget-friendly.

Budget-Friendly Travel: Roaming Without Draining the Bank

Off-Peak Travel: Traveling during off-peak seasons often means lower prices for flights and accommodations.

House-Sitting Opportunities: House-sitting platforms offer opportunities to stay in homes for free in exchange for looking after them. It's a unique way to explore new places on a budget.

Local Adventures: Exploring local attractions and hidden gems can provide a travel experience without the hefty price tag.

Health and Fitness: Staying Well Without Breaking the Bank

Home Workouts: Expensive gym memberships aren't a necessity. Many effective home workout routines require minimal or no equipment.

Generic Medications: Opting for generic versions of medications prescribed by healthcare professionals can lead to substantial savings without compromising health.

Meal Prep for Health and Wealth: Preparing meals at home not only cuts down on dining expenses but also allows for healthier food choices.

Educational Pursuits: Expanding Knowledge on a Budget

Online Courses and Certifications: Many reputable platforms offer free or affordable online courses. It's a chance to expand skills without the hefty price tag of traditional education.

Utilize Public Resources: Public libraries and community centers often host free workshops and lectures. It's an opportunity to learn without spending a dime.

DIY Learning Projects: From coding to language learning, embracing DIY learning projects can be both fulfilling and budget-friendly.

Smart Shopping Strategies: Getting More Value for Every Dollar

Cash-Back Credit Cards: Using a cash-back credit card for everyday expenses allows me to earn a percentage back on purchases.

Comparison Shopping: Before making any significant purchase, I'm comparing prices across different retailers to ensure I'm getting the best deal.

Loyalty Programs: Joining loyalty programs for favorite stores can lead to exclusive discounts and perks over time.

Financial Accountability: Tracking and Analyzing Spending Habits

Expense Tracking Apps: Utilizing apps to track expenses provides a clear picture of where my money is going and where I can make adjustments.

Monthly Financial Reviews: Regularly reviewing my financial goals and progress ensures I stay on track and motivated to continue the frugal journey.

Reflection and Adjustment: Periodically reflecting on spending habits and making necessary adjustments is a key aspect of maintaining financial well-being.

Thrifty Technology: Navigating the Digital World Wisely

Refurbished Electronics: Purchasing refurbished electronics can save a significant amount without compromising on quality.

Digital Subscription Sharing: Many digital subscriptions allow sharing within a household. Teaming up with family or friends can split the cost.

DIY Tech Repairs: Learning basic tech repairs can extend the lifespan of gadgets and save on repair costs.

Frugal Gift-Giving: Spreading Joy Without Emptying the Wallet

Handmade Gifts: Personalized and handmade gifts often carry more sentimental value than store-bought ones. They also save on the budget.

Regifting Thoughtfully: Regifting isn't taboo if done thoughtfully. It's about passing along items that would genuinely be appreciated by the recipient.

Experiences Over Things: Opting for experiences over material gifts can create lasting memories without a hefty price tag.

Sustainable Living: Eco-Friendly Choices That Save Money

Reusable Everything: Investing in reusable items, from water bottles to shopping bags, not only reduces environmental impact but also cuts down on recurring expenses.

DIY Cleaning Products: Creating homemade cleaning products from simple ingredients is not only eco-friendly but also cost-effective.

Second-Hand Furniture: Furnishing a home with second-hand furniture not only saves money but also contributes to sustainable living.

Financial Collaboration: Exploring Group Saving Opportunities

Group Buying Discounts: Joining forces with friends or family for group buying opportunities can unlock bulk discounts.

Community Gardens: Participating in community gardens allows sharing the cost of gardening tools and seeds, creating a communal approach to sustainable living.

Shared Resources: Sharing rarely used items with neighbors or friends, from lawnmowers to power tools, reduces individual expenses.

Flexible Entertainment Subscriptions: Maximizing Value for Money

Rotating Subscriptions: Instead of maintaining multiple streaming or entertainment subscriptions simultaneously, I'm rotating them based on content availability.

Family Plans: Opting for family plans for streaming services or other subscriptions can be more cost-effective when shared among family members or friends.

Trial Period Optimization: Taking advantage of free trial periods for entertainment services allows me to explore content without committing to long-term costs.

Minimalist Living: Embracing Simplicity for Financial Freedom

Declutter and Sell: Decluttering not only simplifies my living space but also provides an opportunity to sell items I no longer need.

Capsule Wardrobe: Creating a capsule wardrobe with versatile pieces reduces the need for frequent clothing purchases and enhances a minimalist lifestyle.

Digital Detox: Reducing digital subscriptions, apps, and services to essential ones minimizes digital clutter and subscription costs.

Financial Independence Planning: Investing for the Future

Automated Investments: Setting up automated contributions to investment accounts ensures consistent and disciplined saving for the future.

Diversified Investments: Diversifying investments across different asset classes minimizes risk and enhances long-term financial stability.

Educational Investment: Investing time in understanding personal finance and investment strategies is as crucial as investing money. Continuous learning lays the foundation for informed decision-making.

Frugal Pet Care: Loving Furry Friends Without Breaking the Bank

DIY Pet Grooming: Learning basic pet grooming skills reduces the need for frequent professional grooming appointments.

Homemade Pet Treats: Creating homemade pet treats from simple ingredients is not only cost-effective but also allows for control over ingredients.

Pet Insurance Research: Researching and choosing the right pet insurance plan can save on unexpected veterinary expenses in the long run.

Repurposing and Upcycling: Breathing New Life Into Items

Repurposing Clothing: Transforming old clothing items into new styles or repurposing them for different uses extends their lifespan.

Furniture Makeovers: Instead of buying new furniture, giving old pieces a makeover with paint or new hardware can freshen up the look.

DIY Home Decor: Creating homemade home decor items using recycled materials adds a personal touch to living spaces without spending a fortune.

Creative Transportation Alternatives: Navigating Without a Car

Car-Sharing Services: Utilizing car-sharing services for occasional transportation needs can be more cost-effective than owning a vehicle.

Biking for Commuting: Choosing biking as a mode of commuting not only saves on transportation costs but also contributes to physical fitness.

Walking for Short Distances: Opting for walking instead of using transportation for short distances not only saves money but also promotes a healthy lifestyle.

Savings Challenges: Making Frugality a Game

No-Spend Challenges: Designating specific days or weeks as "no-spend" challenges encourages mindful spending and boosts savings.

52-Week Money Challenge: Gradually increasing savings over 52 weeks creates a manageable yet impactful savings habit.

Round-Up Apps: Apps that round up everyday purchases to the nearest dollar and invest the spare change contribute to consistent savings over time.

Smartphone Savings Strategies: Maximizing Value for Money

Pre-Owned Phones: Purchasing pre-owned smartphones instead of the latest models significantly reduces upfront costs.

Wi-Fi Calling: Utilizing Wi-Fi calling when available minimizes the need for expensive cellular plans, especially when traveling internationally.

App Consolidation: Streamlining apps and services on the smartphone to essential ones reduces subscription costs and digital clutter.

Educational Freebies: Accessing Knowledge Without Cost

Free Online Courses: Many reputable institutions offer free online courses on various subjects, providing an opportunity for continuous learning without financial investment.

Public Library Events: Public libraries often host free workshops, lectures, and events, expanding access to knowledge and culture without cost.

Open Educational Resources: Leveraging open educational resources for academic and professional development reduces the need for expensive textbooks and courses.

Mindful Eating Practices: Balancing Health and Budget

Intermittent Fasting: Incorporating intermittent fasting not only offers potential health benefits but also reduces the frequency of meals and snacks, contributing to lower food expenses.

Plant-Based Meals: Introducing more plant-based meals into the diet can be both cost-effective and beneficial for health.

Home Gardening: Cultivating a small home garden provides fresh produce at a lower cost and encourages sustainable eating practices.

Flexible Work Arrangements: Optimizing Work-Related Expenses

Telecommuting Options: Negotiating telecommuting options with employers reduces commuting costs and offers flexibility in work arrangements.

Co-Working Spaces: Utilizing co-working spaces or shared office spaces when necessary provides a professional work environment without the long-term commitment of a traditional office.

Professional Development from Home: Exploring professional development opportunities online reduces the need for expensive conferences and workshops.

DIY Beauty Products: Budget-Friendly Self-Care

Homemade Skincare: Creating skincare products at home using natural ingredients minimizes the need for expensive commercial products.

DIY Hair Treatments: Making hair treatments from kitchen ingredients can be an effective and budget-friendly alternative to salon visits.

Minimalist Beauty Routine: Simplifying the beauty routine reduces the need for an extensive array of products, saving both money and time.

Community Sharing Initiatives: Collaborative Savings

Tool Libraries: Utilizing tool libraries in the community allows access to rarely used tools without the need for individual ownership.

Community Gardens: Participating in community gardens not only promotes sustainable living but also provides access to fresh produce at a lower cost.

Skill Exchange Networks: Joining skill exchange networks allows community members to share expertise and services without monetary transactions.

Financial Accountability Partnerships: Mutual Support for Frugality

Frugality Buddies: Partnering with a frugality buddy provides mutual support, motivation, and accountability in pursuing financial goals.

Group Saving Goals: Setting collective saving goals with friends or family encourages collaborative efforts toward shared financial objectives.

Budget Review Sessions: Regularly reviewing budgets with a financial accountability partner provides fresh perspectives and identifies areas for improvement.

Mindful Technology Use: Reducing Unnecessary Expenses

App Deletion Challenges: Periodically deleting unnecessary apps and digital subscriptions for a set period encourages mindful technology use and reveals potential areas for savings.

Digital Detox Days: Designating specific days as digital detox days not only promotes mental well-being but also reduces the temptation for online purchases.

Subscription Audits: Conducting regular audits of digital subscriptions identifies and cancels services that are no longer essential.

Philanthropic Budgeting: Giving Back Within Means

Budget for Charity: Allocating a small portion of the budget for charitable contributions supports meaningful causes without compromising overall financial health.

Volunteer Contributions: Offering time and skills through volunteer work provides a way to contribute to the community without a financial burden.

Community Support Initiatives: Supporting local community initiatives, such as food banks or educational programs, within budgetary constraints contributes to the well-being of the community.

There you have it – an extensive list of 102 creative and detailed ways to cut expenses and master the art of frugality. Remember, frugality isn't about deprivation; it's about making intentional choices that align with your values and financial goals. Pick and choose the strategies that resonate with you, and let the journey to financial mastery begin!

Chapter 4- DIY Frugality

Welcome to the heart of frugal living, where the mantra is not just about saving money but also about embracing the DIY spirit in every aspect of life. In this chapter, we'll embark on a journey to explore the vast realm of do-it-yourself frugality – a world where resourcefulness meets creativity, and every penny saved is a victory. Get ready to dive into the details as we explore how to craft a thrifty lifestyle from scratch, covering everything from home projects to personal care.

1. DIY Home Projects: Transforming Spaces on a Budget

Furniture Revamp:

Let's start with the heartbeat of any home – furniture. Rather than shelling out big bucks for new pieces, consider revamping what you already have. Sanding, painting, or reupholstering can breathe new life into worn-out furniture. Platforms like YouTube and Pinterest are treasure troves of tutorials to guide you through each step.

Repurposing and Upcycling:

Think beyond the conventional uses of items. Turn that vintage ladder into a bookshelf, transform wine crates into storage, or repurpose an old door into a stylish table.

Upcycling not only saves money but also adds a unique touch to your living space.

DIY Home Decor:

Who says you need to splurge on fancy decor items? Create your own wall art, decorative cushions, or even customized curtains. With a bit of creativity and some basic crafting supplies, you can infuse your home with personality without breaking the bank.

Energy-Efficient Improvements:

Improve your home's energy efficiency with simple DIY projects. Seal drafts, add weather stripping, and install energy-efficient light bulbs. These projects not only save money on utility bills but also contribute to a more sustainable lifestyle.

Gardening and Landscaping:

Transform your outdoor space with a green thumb. Grow your own vegetables, herbs, and flowers. DIY landscaping projects like building raised beds, creating a compost bin, or designing a budget-friendly patio can enhance your outdoor oasis without draining your wallet.

2. DIY Personal Care: Nourishing Body and Mind on a Budget

Homemade Skincare:

Bid farewell to expensive skincare products and embrace the simplicity of homemade alternatives. From facial masks to moisturizers, many skincare products can be crafted using natural ingredients like honey, yogurt, and essential oils. Not only are these DIY solutions budget-friendly, but they also allow you to tailor products to your specific skin needs.

DIY Hair Care:

Treat your tresses without the hefty salon price tag. Create your own hair masks, conditioners, and styling products using ingredients like coconut oil, aloe vera, and herbal infusions. Experimenting with DIY hair care not only saves money but also lets you control the ingredients going into your products.

Simple Fitness Routine:

You don't need an expensive gym membership to stay fit. Craft a simple yet effective fitness routine at home using bodyweight exercises, yoga, or low-cost workout equipment. Online platforms offer a plethora of free workout resources, making it easy to stay active without emptying your wallet.

Budget-Friendly Wardrobe:

Revamp your wardrobe without a shopping spree. Learn basic sewing skills to repair and alter clothing. Experiment with tie-dye, embroidery, or fabric paint to breathe new life into old garments. Thrift stores and clothing swaps are also excellent sources for affordable and unique fashion finds.

Mindful Eating Practices:

Take control of your diet without overspending. Embrace meal prepping to save time and money. Plan your meals around budget-friendly staples like rice, beans, and seasonal produce. Experiment with simple yet nutritious recipes to elevate your culinary skills without breaking the bank.

3. DIY Household Essentials: Creating Everyday Necessities from Scratch

Homemade Cleaning Products:

Bid farewell to commercial cleaners and whip up your own cleaning solutions using basic ingredients like vinegar, baking soda, and essential oils. Not only are these DIY cleaners effective, but they also eliminate the need for purchasing multiple specialized products.

DIY Laundry Detergent:

Cut down on laundry costs by making your own detergent. Basic recipes often include ingredients like washing soda, borax, and grated soap. Not only is this a budget-friendly alternative, but it also allows you to control the ingredients, making it suitable for those with sensitive skin.

Candle Making and Air Fresheners:

Create a cozy atmosphere without splurging on scented candles. Learn the art of candle making using affordable materials like soy wax and essential oils. Craft your own air fresheners using baking soda and essential oils to keep your home smelling delightful on a budget.

Homemade Bread and Staples:

Skip the grocery store for basic staples and make your own. From baking your own bread to crafting pantry staples like granola, pasta, and even condiments, DIY kitchen projects not only save money but also provide a sense of accomplishment.

Upcycled Storage Solutions:

Organize your space without investing in pricey storage solutions. Repurpose old crates, baskets, or jars to create stylish and functional storage. DIY shelving units, pegboards, and hooks can transform your space into an organized haven without a hefty price tag.

4. DIY Financial Tools: Taking Control of Your Money Matters

Homemade Budgeting Tools:

Craft personalized budgeting tools that cater to your financial needs. From simple spreadsheets to handmade expense trackers, creating your own budgeting tools allows for customization and a deeper understanding of your financial habits.

DIY Debt Repayment Plans:

Take charge of your debt repayment journey with a DIY plan. Craft a debt snowball or debt avalanche strategy tailored to your financial situation. Utilize free resources and apps to track your progress and stay motivated on your path to financial freedom.

Frugal Investing Strategies:

Explore DIY investment strategies to grow your wealth. Learn the basics of stock market investing, real estate, or other investment avenues through online resources and books. Taking a hands-on approach to investing can reduce reliance on expensive financial advisors.

Savings Challenges:

Craft your own savings challenges to meet your financial goals. Whether it's a no-spend month, a savings jar challenge, or a customized 52-week savings plan, DIY savings challenges provide a tangible and motivating way to build your financial reserves.

Financial Education Initiatives:

Become your own financial educator by curating a DIY learning plan. Utilize free online courses, books, and podcasts to enhance your financial literacy. Understanding investment strategies, budgeting techniques, and economic principles empowers you to make informed financial decisions.

5. DIY Entertainment: Crafting Memorable Experiences on a Budget

DIY Home Entertainment:

Transform your living space into a haven of entertainment without splurging on pricey activities. Host movie nights with homemade popcorn, create a DIY game night, or organize a potluck dinner with friends. Homemade fun not only saves money but also fosters meaningful connections.

Creative Hobbies on a Budget:

Discover budget-friendly hobbies that ignite your passion without burning a hole in your pocket. From drawing and painting to learning a musical instrument, countless DIY hobby options can be explored using online tutorials and community resources.

Local Adventures:

Explore your local community without the need for a lavish vacation. Discover hiking trails, visit local museums on free entry days, or attend community events and festivals. DIY adventures not only save on travel expenses but also foster a deeper connection with your surroundings.

DIY Gifts and Celebrations:

Celebrate special occasions with a personal touch. Craft homemade gifts, create personalized cards, or organize a potluck celebration. DIY celebrations not only save money but also convey thoughtfulness and effort.

DIY Travel Planning:

Plan your own travel adventures without relying on expensive travel agencies. Utilize online resources to find budget-friendly accommodations, explore local transportation options, and discover hidden gems. DIY travel planning allows for flexibility and customization based on your preferences.

6. DIY Learning and Skill Development: Cultivating Knowledge on a Budget

Free Online Courses:

Embark on a journey of continuous learning with free online courses. Platforms like Coursera, edX, and Khan Academy offer a plethora of courses spanning various subjects. Craft your own curriculum tailored to your interests and career goals.

Utilizing Public Libraries:

Explore the wealth of knowledge available at your local library. From books and audiobooks to workshops and lectures, public libraries provide a budget-friendly avenue for self-education. Craft your own reading list and make the library a regular destination for intellectual exploration.

DIY Learning Projects:

Embark on hands-on learning projects to develop practical skills. From coding and graphic design to home repair and gardening, DIY learning projects provide a tangible way to acquire new abilities without the hefty price tag of formal education.

7. DIY Health and Wellness: Nurturing Well-Being on a Budget

Home Workouts:

Stay fit without the need for an expensive gym membership. Craft your own home workout routine using online resources and free fitness apps. Utilize bodyweight exercises, yoga, or affordable home gym equipment to prioritize your physical well-being.

Mindful Eating Practices:

Take control of your nutrition with mindful eating practices. Experiment with meal prepping, plant-based meals, and home gardening to not only save on food expenses but also foster a healthier lifestyle. DIY nutrition allows for customization based on your dietary preferences and health goals.

DIY Mental Health Practices:

Prioritize mental well-being with DIY mental health practices. Explore meditation, mindfulness, and journaling as cost-effective tools for stress management. Crafting your own mental health toolkit allows for tailored strategies that resonate with your unique needs.

Natural Remedies and DIY Healthcare:

Explore natural remedies and DIY healthcare practices to address common ailments. From herbal teas and homemade salves to DIY first aid kits, cultivating your own healthcare solutions not only saves money but also promotes a holistic approach to well-being.

8. DIY Sustainable Living: Navigating an Eco-Friendly Lifestyle on a Budget

Zero-Waste DIY Initiatives:

Embrace a zero-waste lifestyle with DIY initiatives. Create your own reusable shopping bags, produce bags, and beeswax wraps. Explore DIY household items like cleaning cloths and dish scrubbers to reduce reliance on disposable alternatives.

Sustainable Gardening Practices:

Cultivate a sustainable garden by embracing eco-friendly practices. Implement composting, rainwater harvesting, and natural pest control methods. DIY sustainable gardening not only contributes to environmental conservation but also provides a source of fresh produce.

Upcycled Fashion and Accessories:

Craft a sustainable wardrobe by upcycling old clothing and accessories. Transform outdated pieces into stylish garments or repurpose fabrics into new accessories. DIY upcycled fashion not only reduces textile waste but also allows for a unique and environmentally conscious style.

Sustainable DIY Home:

Transform your living space into an eco-friendly haven with sustainable DIY projects. From creating your own cleaning products to implementing energy-efficient improvements, DIY sustainability not only reduces environmental impact but also leads to long-term cost savings.

In this comprehensive exploration of DIY frugality, we've delved into the essence of crafting a thrifty lifestyle from scratch. From home projects to personal care, financial tools to entertainment, learning to health and wellness, and finally, sustainable living – the DIY frugality journey is a multifaceted approach to living intentionally, creatively, and economically. Remember, each DIY endeavor is not just a cost-saving measure; it's a step towards a more self-reliant, sustainable, and fulfilling life. As you embark on your own DIY frugality adventure, may creativity be your guide and resourcefulness your companion.

Chapter 5- Frugal Living Beyond the Basics

Welcome to the pinnacle of frugal living, where we delve into advanced strategies that go beyond the basics. In this chapter, we'll explore the intricacies of mastering frugality, covering everything from advanced budgeting techniques to sophisticated investment strategies. Get ready to elevate your financial game as we unravel the layers of frugal living beyond the ordinary.

1. Advanced Budgeting Techniques: Precision in Financial Planning

Zero-Based Budgeting:

Take your budgeting skills to the next level with zero-based budgeting. Every dollar has a purpose, and no money is left unallocated. This technique ensures that every aspect of your income is assigned to specific categories, leaving no room for financial ambiguity.

Envelope System 2.0:

Revamp the classic envelope system by integrating it with digital tools. Use budgeting apps to allocate virtual envelopes for different spending categories. This modern adaptation retains the essence of cash-only spending while offering the convenience of digital transactions.

Dynamic Budget Adjustments:

Master the art of dynamic budgeting by adjusting your spending plan in real-time. Factor in unexpected expenses, windfalls, or changes in income promptly. This proactive approach ensures that your budget remains a fluid and responsive financial tool.

Periodic Financial Reviews:

Elevate your financial acumen by conducting periodic reviews of your budget. Analyze your spending patterns, identify areas for improvement, and adjust your budget accordingly. Regular financial reviews empower you to make informed decisions and stay on track with your financial goals.

2. Advanced Savings Strategies: Building Wealth with Precision

High-Yield Savings Accounts:

Move beyond traditional savings accounts and explore high-yield options. These accounts offer higher interest rates, allowing your money to work harder for you. Research and compare different accounts to find the best fit for your financial goals.

Certificates of Deposit (CDs):

Diversify your savings portfolio by incorporating Certificates of Deposit. CDs provide higher interest rates than regular savings accounts, with the trade-off of a fixed term. Strategically use CDs to lock in higher returns for specific savings goals.

Investment-Linked Savings:

Explore savings accounts linked to investments, combining the benefits of savings and investing. These accounts often offer the potential for higher returns than traditional savings accounts while providing some level of liquidity.

Automatic Escalation Savings:

Implement an automatic escalation feature in your savings plan. Gradually increase the amount you contribute to your savings or investment accounts over time. This strategy ensures that your savings grow in tandem with your income.

3. Advanced Investing Strategies: Navigating the Financial Markets

Dividend Growth Investing:

Shift your focus to dividends by adopting a dividend growth investing strategy. Invest in companies with a history of increasing dividend payouts. Over time, the compounding effect of growing dividends can significantly enhance your investment returns.

Tax-Efficient Investing:

Optimize your investment strategy with a focus on tax efficiency. Explore tax-advantaged accounts, tax-loss harvesting, and strategic asset allocation to minimize your tax liabilities and maximize your after-tax returns.

Sector Rotation:

Fine-tune your investment portfolio by practicing sector rotation. Capitalize on market trends by adjusting your holdings to align with sectors poised for growth. This advanced strategy requires continuous market analysis and a deep understanding of economic cycles.

Alternative Investments:

Diversify your investment portfolio by exploring alternative investments. Consider real estate, commodities, or peer-to-peer lending as avenues for potential returns beyond traditional stocks and bonds. Conduct thorough research and assess risk before venturing into alternative investments.

4. Advanced Debt Management: Conquering Debt Strategically

Debt Snowflake Method:

Enhance your debt repayment strategy with the debt snowflake method. This approach involves making small, additional payments whenever you have extra funds. These micro-payments contribute to faster debt reduction over time.

Debt Laddering:

Organize and prioritize your debts with the debt laddering technique. Rank your debts based on interest rates, and focus on paying off high-interest debts first. As each debt is cleared, redirect the freed-up funds to tackle the next one in line.

Debt Consolidation Strategies:

Consider debt consolidation strategies to streamline your repayment process. Explore options like balance transfers, personal loans, or debt consolidation programs. This advanced approach can simplify your debt landscape and potentially reduce overall interest costs.

Negotiating Lower Interest Rates:

Master the art of negotiation to secure lower interest rates on your debts. Contact creditors, explain your financial situation, and request a rate reduction. A lower interest rate can significantly accelerate your debt payoff journey.

5. Advanced Frugal Living Hacks: Fine-Tuning Your Lifestyle

Geoarbitrage:

Explore the concept of geoarbitrage by strategically relocating to areas with lower living costs. This advanced frugal living hack allows you to maintain or improve your quality of life while benefiting from a more budget-friendly environment.

Credit Card Hacking:

Navigate the world of credit card rewards with advanced credit card hacking techniques. Maximize cashback, travel rewards, and other perks by strategically using multiple credit cards. This approach requires meticulous planning and disciplined financial management.

Advanced Couponing Strategies:

Elevate your couponing skills by mastering advanced strategies. Combine manufacturer coupons with store promotions, utilize cashback apps, and explore stacking opportunities. This sophisticated approach can result in significant savings on your regular expenses.

Rent Hacking:

Optimize your housing costs through rent hacking. Negotiate rent prices, explore roommate or co-living arrangements, or consider house hacking by renting out a portion of your living space. This advanced frugal living strategy can unlock substantial savings on your housing expenses.

6. Advanced Career and Income Strategies: Maximizing Earning Potential

Side Business Optimization:

If you have a side business or freelance gig, optimize its earning potential. Explore additional revenue streams within your niche, implement efficient business processes, and invest in marketing strategies to expand your client base.

Professional Development Investments:

Invest in your professional development strategically. Identify high-impact skills or certifications that can significantly boost your earning potential. This advanced approach involves a calculated investment in your own skill set to open doors to higher-paying opportunities.

Negotiating Higher Salaries:

Master the art of salary negotiation to secure higher compensation. Conduct thorough research on industry standards, showcase your accomplishments, and confidently negotiate for a salary that reflects your skills and contributions.

Passive Income Portfolio:

Build a diversified passive income portfolio to supplement your primary income. Explore investments that generate ongoing returns, such as dividends, rental income, or royalties. This advanced income strategy requires careful planning and a long-term perspective.

7. Advanced Financial Planning: Orchestrating Your Financial Symphony

Family Financial Planning:

Elevate your financial planning to encompass your entire family. Establish financial goals, create a comprehensive budget, and coordinate investment strategies. This advanced approach ensures that your family's financial well-being is orchestrated harmoniously.

Generational Wealth Building:

Shift your focus to generational wealth building by implementing strategies that extend beyond your lifetime. Explore trusts, estate planning, and educational funds to create a lasting financial legacy for future generations.

Early Retirement Strategies:

Craft an early retirement plan that aligns with your financial goals and lifestyle aspirations. Consider factors such as the 4% rule, healthcare planning, and potential income streams during retirement. This advanced strategy requires meticulous preparation and a clear vision for your post-retirement life.

Advanced Tax Planning:

Optimize your tax strategy with advanced tax planning techniques. Leverage tax-efficient investments, explore tax credits and deductions, and consider working with a tax professional to ensure that your financial decisions align with your tax goals.

8. Advanced Lifestyle Optimization: Balancing Quality of Life and Frugality

Intentional Spending:

Practice intentional spending by aligning your expenses with your values and long-term goals. Identify areas where spending brings true joy and fulfillment, and allocate resources accordingly. This advanced frugal living approach emphasizes quality over quantity.

Mindful Minimalism:

Elevate minimalism to a mindful level by curating a lifestyle that prioritizes experiences over possessions. Integrate minimalist principles into various aspects of your life, from decluttering physical spaces to simplifying digital environments. This advanced approach fosters a sense of clarity and purpose.

Purposeful Philanthropy:

Infuse purpose into your philanthropic efforts by aligning charitable contributions with your values. Research and support causes that resonate with you on a personal level. This advanced approach ensures that your philanthropic endeavors have a meaningful and lasting impact.

Digital Detox and Mental Wellness:

Consciously manage your digital consumption to optimize mental well-being. Implement periodic digital detoxes, establish healthy boundaries with technology, and prioritize activities that nurture mental wellness. This advanced frugal living strategy emphasizes the importance of a balanced and mindful lifestyle.

As we explore the realm of advanced frugal living, remember that financial mastery is a journey, not a destination. These advanced strategies are tools to help you refine your approach, navigate complex financial landscapes, and achieve a level of financial well-being that aligns with your aspirations. As you integrate these advanced techniques into your frugal living toolkit, may your financial journey be both enriching and fulfilling.

Chapter 6- Stress-Free Frugal Living

In this chapter, we'll explore the art of harmonizing frugality with a serene lifestyle, allowing you to navigate your financial journey with peace of mind. From mindfulness practices to simplifying routines, we'll delve into the depths of stress-free frugal living, where financial harmony meets inner tranquility.

1. Mindful Budgeting: Finding Calm in Financial Planning

Breathing Life into Numbers:

Transform budgeting from a stressful task into a mindful practice. Approach your budget with a calm and centered mindset. Breathe life into the numbers by visualizing your financial goals and the intentional choices that lead to them.

Simplicity in Financial Tracking:

Simplify your financial tracking methods. Embrace minimalist spreadsheets or budgeting apps that align with your preferred level of detail. The key is to streamline the process, allowing you to focus on the big picture without feeling overwhelmed by intricate details.

Gratitude Budgeting:

Infuse your budgeting process with gratitude. Reflect on the abundance in your life, even in the midst of financial goals. This mindfulness technique not only reduces stress but also helps shift your mindset towards contentment and appreciation.

2. Tranquil Saving Strategies: Building Wealth at Your Own Pace

Slow and Steady Wins the Savings Race:

Adopt a slow and steady approach to saving. Instead of chasing rapid results, cultivate a tranquil mindset that values consistency over intensity. This approach allows you to build wealth at a pace that aligns with your stress tolerance and financial well-being.

Savings as a Form of Self-Care:

Reframe the act of saving as a form of self-care. Just as you invest time in activities that nourish your well-being, allocate financial resources to your savings. This stress-free perspective transforms saving from a burden to a nurturing practice.

Peaceful Emergency Fund Building:

Build your emergency fund with a sense of peace. Set realistic milestones and celebrate each achievement. Knowing that you have a financial safety net contributes to a stress-free mindset, allowing you to navigate unexpected challenges with resilience.

3. Calm Investing: Navigating Financial Markets with Serenity

Long-Term Vision:

Adopt a long-term vision when it comes to investing. Embrace the tranquility that comes from understanding that short-term market fluctuations are a natural part of the journey. Focus on the enduring growth potential of your investments.

Stress-Free Diversification:

Diversify your investment portfolio with a stress-free mindset. Instead of chasing the latest trends, calmly spread your investments across different asset classes. Diversification acts as a shield against market volatility, providing a serene foundation for your financial future.

Automated Peace:

Automate your investment contributions for a stress-free experience. Set up automatic transfers to your investment accounts, allowing you to stay consistent without the need for constant manual intervention. This hands-off approach fosters financial well-being and tranquility.

4. Zen Debt Management: Cultivating Peace on the Repayment Journey

Non-Judgmental Self-Reflection:

Approach debt repayment with non-judgmental self-reflection. Rather than viewing debt as a source of stress, acknowledge it as a temporary aspect of your financial journey. Cultivate a mindset of self-compassion, recognizing that everyone faces unique challenges.

One Step at a Time:

Break down debt repayment into manageable steps. Whether using the debt snowball or debt avalanche method, focus on one debt at a time. This gradual approach fosters a stress-free mindset, allowing you to celebrate small victories along the way.

Financial Forgiveness:

Practice financial forgiveness on your debt repayment journey. Release any guilt or shame associated with past financial decisions. Embrace the present moment and make choices that align with your current financial goals. This forgiving mindset contributes to stress reduction.

5. Minimalist Frugality: Embracing Simplicity for Inner Calm

Simplicity in Consumer Choices:

Cultivate simplicity in your consumer choices. Embrace minimalist frugality by consciously selecting items that add value to your life. This intentional approach reduces decision fatigue and contributes to a serene living environment.

Decluttering for Mental Clarity:

Engage in decluttering not just as a physical task but as a mental practice. Clearing physical spaces of unnecessary items fosters mental clarity and tranquility. The simplicity that arises from decluttering extends to your financial mindset.

Contentment in Frugal Living:

Find contentment in frugal living. Shift your focus from external validations to internal fulfillment. The ability to derive joy from simple pleasures and mindful spending choices contributes to a stress-free frugal lifestyle.

6. Holistic Wellness on a Budget: Nurturing Mind and Body

Mindful Eating Practices:

Nourish your body and mind through mindful eating practices. Embrace a balanced and budget-friendly approach to nutrition. Pay attention to your body's signals, savor each bite, and foster a positive relationship with food.

Affordable Wellness Routines:

Craft affordable wellness routines that align with your values. From home workouts to meditation practices, explore budget-friendly options that contribute to your overall well-being. The synergy of physical and mental health fosters a stress-free lifestyle.

Nature as a Healing Space:

Tap into the healing power of nature on a budget. Spend time in green spaces, embark on budget-friendly hikes, or create a small outdoor sanctuary at home. Connecting with nature is a powerful stress-relief tool.

7. Time Wealth: Prioritizing Time for Lasting Happiness

Intentional Time Budgeting:

Budget your time with intention, just as you budget your finances. Prioritize activities that align with your values and contribute to your overall well-being. This intentional time budgeting fosters a sense of fulfillment and reduces the stress of overcommitment.

Quality Over Quantity:

Embrace a quality-over-quantity mindset in your activities. Rather than filling your schedule with numerous tasks, focus on fewer activities that bring genuine joy and satisfaction. This approach enhances the quality of your experiences.

Mindful Technology Use:

Establish mindful boundaries with technology to reclaim time wealth. Designate specific periods for digital detox, limit screen time, and cultivate presence in your daily activities. Mindful technology use contributes to a sense of balance and stress reduction.

8. Compassionate Financial Self-Care: Nurturing the Relationship with Yourself

Financial Self-Reflection:

Engage in financial self-reflection with compassion. Understand the emotions and beliefs tied to your financial decisions. Approach your financial journey with a sense of curiosity and self-acceptance, fostering a compassionate relationship with money.

Regular Financial Check-Ins:

Conduct regular financial check-ins with a compassionate mindset. Rather than viewing them as assessments, consider them opportunities for self-care. Celebrate progress, adjust goals with kindness, and navigate challenges with resilience.

Rewarding Frugal Milestones:

Celebrate frugal milestones with self-rewards. Acknowledge the achievements on your financial journey, whether big or small, with gestures of self-appreciation. This practice reinforces positive financial habits and contributes to a stress-free relationship with money.

As we journey into the realm of stress-free frugal living, remember that financial well-being is inseparable from inner tranquility. By intertwining mindfulness with frugality, you embark on a path where financial decisions become a source of peace rather than stress. May this exploration guide you towards a serene financial existence, where the pursuit of financial goals is harmonized with the pursuit of a content and fulfilled life.

Chapter 7- Frugal Living Family

In this chapter, we will explore the intricate dynamics of adopting frugal living as a family lifestyle. From instilling financial values in children to navigating shared financial goals, get ready to embark on a journey where frugality becomes a collective endeavor, fostering resilience, unity, and lasting financial well-being.

**1. Foundations of Frugal Family Values:

Family values serve as the cornerstone of a frugal living lifestyle. Establishing a shared set of financial principles lays the groundwork for collective decision-making and fosters a sense of unity. Explore and articulate the values that underpin your family's approach to money, such as sustainability, resourcefulness, and mindful consumption.

Instilling Financial Literacy in Children:

Nurturing financial literacy in children is a powerful investment in their future. Introduce age-appropriate financial concepts, involve them in family budget discussions, and encourage responsible money management. Create a positive and educational environment that equips them with essential life skills.

Family Meetings for Financial Planning:

Initiate regular family meetings to discuss financial goals, challenges, and decisions. These gatherings provide an opportunity for open communication, shared decision-making, and the cultivation of a collaborative financial mindset. Encourage every family member, regardless of age, to actively participate in these discussions.

2. Budgeting as a Family Practice:

Extend the concept of budgeting to a family-wide endeavor. Collaboratively create a family budget that aligns with your shared financial goals. Involve each family member in decision-making processes, allowing them to understand the trade-offs and priorities involved in managing the family's finances.

Teaching Financial Responsibility:

Empower children with a sense of financial responsibility from an early age. Assign age-appropriate financial tasks, such as saving a portion of their allowance or contributing to family goals. This hands-on experience instills a sense of ownership and accountability in their financial decisions.

Family Savings Goals:

Set collective savings goals as a family. Whether it's saving for a family vacation, a special purchase, or an emergency fund, involve everyone in the process. Celebrate milestones together, reinforcing the idea that financial achievements are a result of collaborative efforts.

Financial Challenges as Learning Opportunities:

Approach financial challenges as valuable learning opportunities for the family. When faced with budget constraints or unexpected expenses, engage in open discussions about potential solutions. Encourage creativity and problem-solving skills, teaching resilience in the face of financial uncertainties.

3. Frugal Family Meal Planning:

Meal planning becomes a collaborative and cost-effective family activity. Involve family members in creating weekly meal plans, grocery shopping, and even cooking. Emphasize the importance of mindful eating and minimizing food waste. Not only does this foster frugality, but it also promotes shared responsibilities and teamwork.

Cooking and Eating Together:

Transform cooking and eating into communal activities. Engage in family cooking sessions where everyone contributes to the meal preparation. Shared meals strengthen familial bonds while reinforcing the financial wisdom of home-cooked meals over restaurant dining.

Budget-Friendly Recipes and Tips:

Explore budget-friendly recipes and cooking tips as a family. Experiment with cost-effective ingredients, learn about bulk cooking, and discover ways to repurpose leftovers creatively. This culinary journey not only supports frugality but also encourages a sense of culinary exploration within the family.

Gardening as a Family Project:

Consider starting a family garden as a sustainable and budget-friendly project. Engage children in planting, caring for, and harvesting fruits, vegetables, or herbs. This hands-on experience instills an appreciation for nature, encourages healthy eating, and provides a tangible connection to the sources of food.

4. Family-Focused Frugal Entertainment:

Reimagine family entertainment through frugal and enriching activities. From movie nights at home to DIY arts and crafts, explore affordable options that prioritize quality time over extravagant expenses. Engaging in such activities not only strengthens family bonds but also reinforces the notion that meaningful experiences need not come with a hefty price tag.

DIY Family Game Nights:

Host DIY family game nights with board games, card games, or even homemade games. This cost-effective and entertaining activity brings the family together for laughter and friendly competition. Rotate the responsibility of choosing games, allowing each family member to contribute to the fun.

Nature Walks and Outdoor Adventures:

Explore the beauty of nature as a family. Embark on budget-friendly nature walks, hikes, or picnics in local parks. Connecting with the outdoors not only provides a refreshing change of scenery but also encourages physical activity and environmental appreciation.

Library Excursions and Book Clubs:

Transform the local library into a family haven for knowledge and entertainment. Regular library excursions can become a shared ritual, fostering a love for reading and learning. Consider starting a family book club, where each member selects a book for the family to read and discuss.

5. Educational Frugality for Family Growth:

Leverage frugality as a tool for continuous family growth and education. Encourage a culture of learning, exploration, and skill development within the family. This commitment to education not only enhances individual capabilities but also reinforces the family's collective ability to adapt and thrive in various circumstances.

Shared Learning Goals:

Establish shared learning goals as a family. Whether it's acquiring a new skill, learning a language, or exploring a subject of mutual interest, set targets that everyone can work towards. This collaborative approach fosters a sense of intellectual curiosity and achievement.

Utilizing Free and Low-Cost Educational Resources:

Tap into free and low-cost educational resources available online and in your community. From online courses and educational apps to community workshops and events, explore diverse avenues for learning without straining the family budget. Encourage each family member to pursue their unique educational interests.

DIY Educational Projects:

Engage in DIY educational projects that align with family interests. Whether it's building a model, conducting science experiments, or creating a family scrapbook, these hands-on activities provide a fun and cost-effective way to learn together. Celebrate the completion of projects as a family accomplishment.

6. Frugal Family Travel:

Embrace frugal travel as a means of creating lasting family memories. From road trips to budget-friendly destinations, explore travel options that align with your financial goals. The shared experiences gained from frugal travel not only enrich family bonds but also provide a sense of adventure and discovery.

Planning Budget-Friendly Vacations:

Involve the entire family in planning budget-friendly vacations. Research affordable accommodation options, explore local attractions, and find cost-effective ways to experience new destinations. This collaborative approach not only enhances the travel experience but also instills financial prudence in family members.

Camping Adventures:

Consider camping as a frugal and immersive family adventure. Camping trips provide opportunities for outdoor exploration, bonding around a campfire, and appreciating the simplicity of nature. Engage in activities like hiking, fishing, or stargazing, creating cherished memories on a budget.

Staycations and Local Exploration:

Rediscover the charm of your local area through staycations and day trips. Visit nearby parks, museums, or landmarks that you may not have explored before. This frugal approach to exploration encourages a deeper appreciation for the community and surroundings.

7. Financial Communication within the Family:

Foster open and transparent financial communication within the family. Establish an environment where discussions about money are free from judgment or anxiety. Encourage family members to express their financial goals, concerns, and aspirations, promoting a sense of shared responsibility.

Age-Appropriate Financial Conversations:

Tailor financial conversations to the age and understanding level of each family member. Discuss basic financial concepts with younger children and gradually introduce more complex topics as they mature. This age-appropriate approach ensures that financial education is an ongoing and accessible process.

Setting Collective Financial Goals:

Define and work towards collective financial goals as a family. Whether it's saving for a specific purchase, funding education, or achieving a shared milestone, having a common financial objective fosters collaboration and commitment. Regularly revisit and celebrate progress towards these goals.

Conflict Resolution and Financial Harmony:

Equip the family with effective conflict resolution skills related to finances. Address disagreements with empathy, active listening, and a collaborative problem-solving mindset. Cultivate an atmosphere where financial challenges are viewed as opportunities for growth and understanding.

8. Legacy-Building and Generational Wealth:

Elevate your family's financial journey by embracing the concept of generational wealth. Strategically plan for the future and instill values that transcend monetary assets. Explore avenues such as trusts, educational funds, and estate planning to create a lasting legacy that extends beyond the current generation.

Teaching the Value of Giving Back:

Integrate the value of giving back into the family's financial philosophy. Engage in philanthropic activities together, whether through volunteering, supporting local charities, or contributing to meaningful causes. Teaching the importance of generosity and compassion fosters a legacy of positive impact.

Transferring Financial Knowledge:

Pass on financial knowledge from one generation to the next. Create opportunities for older family members to share their financial experiences, lessons learned, and insights with younger generations. This intergenerational transfer of wisdom contributes to the family's financial resilience and unity.

Encouraging Entrepreneurial Spirit:

Nurture an entrepreneurial spirit within the family. Encourage creativity, innovation, and a proactive approach to financial opportunities. Whether it's starting a small family business or pursuing entrepreneurial endeavors individually, instill a mindset that embraces initiative and resourcefulness.

As you embark on the journey of frugal living as a family lifestyle, remember that each step taken together is a building block for lasting financial well-being. Through shared experiences, open communication, and a commitment to growth, your family can thrive on the foundations of frugality, creating a legacy of financial wisdom and unity for generations to come. May this exploration of frugal family living inspire resilience, harmony, and prosperity within your family unit.

Chapter 8- Sustaining Frugal Living Practices

Welcome to the culmination of your frugal living journey, where the focus shifts from initiation to sustainability. In this chapter, we delve into the strategies and principles that will help you not only maintain but thrive in your frugal lifestyle over the long term. From adapting to changing circumstances to refining your frugal toolkit, let's explore the art of sustaining frugal living practices with resilience, mindfulness, and a commitment to lasting financial well-being.

**1. Adapting to Life Changes:

Recognize that life is dynamic, and your frugal living practices should evolve alongside it. Whether you experience changes in income, family structure, or lifestyle, adaptability is key to sustaining your frugal journey. Embrace flexibility in your budget, savings goals, and overall financial approach.

Reassessing Budget and Priorities:

Regularly reassess your budget and financial priorities to align with current circumstances. Life changes may necessitate adjustments to your spending plan, savings goals, and debt repayment strategies. Stay proactive and open to modifying your financial roadmap based on the evolving needs of your life.

Navigating Career Transitions:

Navigate career transitions with a strategic mindset. Whether you're switching jobs, starting a business, or experiencing periods of unemployment, approach these changes with resilience. Adjust your financial plan accordingly, exploring new opportunities for income generation and cost-cutting measures.

Financial Planning for Major Life Events:

Plan for major life events, such as marriage, parenthood, or homeownership, with a frugal perspective. Anticipate the financial implications of these milestones and incorporate them into your long-term financial strategy. Thoughtful planning ensures that you can celebrate these moments without compromising your frugal principles.

2. Resilient Financial Tools:

Build a resilient toolkit of financial strategies that withstand the test of time. These tools serve as pillars supporting your frugal living practices, providing stability and adaptability in the face of economic fluctuations and personal challenges.

Emergency Fund Maintenance:

Regularly assess and replenish your emergency fund to ensure it remains a robust safety net. Aim for three to six months' worth of living expenses, adjusting the target based on your unique circumstances. An adequately funded emergency fund safeguards your financial stability during unforeseen circumstances.

Strategic Debt Management:

Maintain a strategic approach to debt management. Whether you're in the process of paying off debt or using debt strategically for investments, regularly review your debt landscape. Consider refinancing options, explore lower-interest alternatives, and ensure that your debt remains aligned with your overall financial goals.

Investment Diversification:

Diversify your investment portfolio to enhance its resilience. Regularly review your investments, assess risk tolerance, and explore opportunities for diversification. A well-diversified portfolio is better equipped to weather market fluctuations and contribute to long-term financial growth.

Regular Retirement Planning Updates:

Stay proactive in your retirement planning by regularly updating your goals and contributions. Monitor changes in retirement account regulations, assess the performance of your investments, and adjust your strategy as needed. Regular updates ensure that your retirement plan aligns with your evolving financial objectives.

3. Continuous Skill Development:

Cultivate a mindset of continuous skill development to enhance your frugal living capabilities. Acquiring new skills not only contributes to personal growth but also expands your resourcefulness in various aspects of life, from DIY projects to income-generating opportunities.

Learning Practical DIY Skills:

Invest time in learning practical DIY skills that align with your frugal lifestyle. From home repairs to crafting and gardening, acquiring these skills not only reduces reliance on external services but also empowers you to handle various tasks independently.

Expanding Income-Generating Skills:

Identify and cultivate income-generating skills that complement your career or personal interests. This could involve freelancing, consulting, or leveraging your expertise in specific areas. Diversifying your income streams enhances financial stability and provides opportunities for additional savings.

Staying Tech-Savvy:

Embrace technology and stay abreast of digital tools that can optimize your frugal living practices. From budgeting apps to online resources for skill development, leveraging technology enhances your efficiency in managing finances and adapting to the evolving landscape.

Networking for Mutual Benefit:

Cultivate a network of like-minded individuals for mutual support and knowledge exchange. Engage in local or online communities that share frugal living values. Networking provides opportunities to learn from others' experiences, share insights, and build a supportive community.

4. Mindful Consumption Habits:

Deepen your commitment to mindful consumption habits as a cornerstone of sustained frugal living. Develop a heightened awareness of your spending patterns, environmental impact, and overall consumer behavior. Mindful consumption not only reduces expenses but also aligns with sustainable and intentional living.

Evaluating Purchases with Intention:

Before making a purchase, practice intentional evaluation. Ask yourself whether the item aligns with your values, serves a practical purpose, or contributes to your overall well-being. This deliberate approach minimizes impulse buying and fosters a mindful relationship with material possessions.

Embracing Minimalism:

Explore the principles of minimalism as a guiding philosophy for sustained frugal living. Streamline your possessions, focusing on items that bring genuine joy and value. Minimalism not only reduces clutter but also encourages a conscious and deliberate approach to consumption.

Sustainable and Ethical Choices:

Incorporate sustainability and ethics into your consumption choices. Opt for products and services that align with environmental and ethical standards. This conscious decision-making not only supports responsible businesses but also contributes to a more sustainable and compassionate global ecosystem.

Reevaluating Subscription Services:

Regularly reevaluate your subscription services to ensure they align with your current needs and priorities. Eliminate redundant or underutilized subscriptions, freeing up resources for more intentional spending. This practice prevents financial leakage and enhances the efficiency of your budget.

5. Holistic Well-Being Practices:

Prioritize holistic well-being practices that contribute to your physical, mental, and emotional health. A sustained frugal lifestyle encompasses more than just financial considerations; it emphasizes a balanced and fulfilling life.

Exercise and Fitness on a Budget:

Incorporate exercise and fitness into your routine with budget-friendly options. Explore outdoor activities, bodyweight exercises, or home workout routines that don't require expensive gym memberships. Physical well-being is an integral component of sustained frugal living.

Mindfulness and Stress Reduction:

Cultivate mindfulness practices to reduce stress and enhance mental well-being. Incorporate activities such as meditation, deep breathing exercises, or nature walks into your daily routine. These practices not only contribute to a stress-free mindset but also align with the principles of intentional and mindful living.

Quality Sleep and Frugality:

Prioritize quality sleep as a fundamental aspect of sustained frugal living. Establish healthy sleep habits and create a conducive sleep environment without unnecessary expenses. Adequate rest enhances cognitive function, emotional resilience, and overall well-being.

Balanced Nutrition on a Budget:

Maintain balanced nutrition without compromising your budget. Explore cost-effective meal planning, bulk purchasing of staples, and efficient cooking practices. Nourishing your body with wholesome, budget-friendly food choices contributes to sustained physical health.

6. Environmental Consciousness:

Deepen your commitment to environmental consciousness as an integral part of sustained frugal living. Align your practices with eco-friendly principles, reducing waste, and making choices that contribute to a healthier planet.

Reducing Single-Use Plastics:

Minimize the use of single-use plastics by opting for reusable alternatives. Invest in reusable water bottles, shopping bags, and containers. This conscious choice not only reduces environmental impact but also aligns with frugal living by avoiding unnecessary, repetitive expenses.

Energy-Efficient Practices:

Implement energy-efficient practices in your home to reduce utility costs. Explore options such as energy-efficient appliances, smart thermostats, and mindful consumption of electricity. These practices align with frugal living while contributing to a more sustainable lifestyle.

Sustainable Transportation Choices:

Consider sustainable transportation choices to reduce both costs and environmental impact. Explore public transportation, carpooling, biking, or walking as alternatives to individual car use. These choices not only save money on fuel and maintenance but also contribute to reduced carbon emissions.

Zero-Waste Initiatives:

Embrace zero-waste initiatives by minimizing unnecessary packaging and actively participating in recycling programs. Composting, reusing, and repurposing items contribute to a sustainable and frugal approach to consumption. Adopting a zero-waste mindset aligns with the principles of mindful and intentional living.

7. Community Engagement and Contribution:

Foster a sense of community engagement and contribution as a pillar of sustained frugal living. Actively participate in local initiatives, contribute to charitable causes, and share your knowledge and skills with others. Community engagement enhances the social dimension of frugal living and contributes to a sense of purpose.

Volunteering and Skill Sharing:

Explore volunteering opportunities that align with your skills and interests. By sharing your time and expertise, you not only contribute to the community but also create meaningful connections. Volunteering is a frugal way to make a positive impact without relying solely on financial resources.

Local Economy Support:

Prioritize supporting local businesses and the regional economy. Engage in local markets, patronize independent retailers, and participate in community events. This commitment to local engagement fosters a sense of belonging and strengthens the economic resilience of your community.

Educational Initiatives:

Contribute to educational initiatives within your community. Share your knowledge, organize workshops, or participate in community education programs. Empowering others with frugal living skills creates a ripple effect, enhancing the financial well-being of the community as a whole.

8. Reflection, Gratitude, and Future Planning:

Conclude your journey by incorporating reflection, gratitude, and future planning into your sustained frugal living practices. These elements provide a holistic framework for continuous growth, appreciation, and intentional direction.

Reflective Practices:

Engage in reflective practices to assess your frugal living journey. Regularly evaluate your financial goals, choices, and overall well-being. Reflection enhances self-awareness and allows you to make intentional adjustments as needed, ensuring that your frugal living practices remain aligned with your values.

Gratitude as a Daily Ritual:

Cultivate a daily gratitude ritual as a reminder of the abundance in your life. Acknowledge the positive aspects of your frugal living journey, expressing gratitude for the lessons learned, the experiences gained, and the financial stability achieved. Gratitude fosters a positive mindset and reinforces the fulfillment derived from intentional living.

Future Planning with Purpose:

Conclude your sustained frugal living journey by envisioning the future with purpose. Set new financial goals, whether they involve achieving greater savings, pursuing meaningful experiences, or contributing to long-term investments. Future planning ensures that your frugal lifestyle remains dynamic and aligned with your evolving aspirations.

As you embrace the art of sustaining frugal living practices, remember that the journey is as significant as the destination. Through adaptability, continuous learning, and a holistic approach to well-being, you can thrive in a sustained frugal lifestyle. May this exploration guide you towards enduring financial well-being, mindful living, and a future filled with purpose and abundance.

Conclusion

As we wrap up our journey through frugal living, let's think about it like putting the finishing touches on a beautiful painting. This way of life is more than just smart spending; it's about making choices that make our lives better and richer. We've covered a lot - from handling money to living in a way that feels good, and we've seen that frugal living is a path to happiness and purpose.

In our own lives, things can change - jobs, families, and big moments. But frugal living isn't about dealing with these changes; it's about using them to grow and get better. The tools we've talked about, like having money set aside for emergencies and learning new skills, help us handle whatever comes our way.

Living frugally isn't just about having less; it's about being creative and resourceful. Each small choice we make, like buying less stuff and finding joy in experiences, adds up to a life that feels full and meaningful.

Looking ahead, being thankful for what we've learned and the moments we've enjoyed keeps us focused on what really matters. And when we share what we've learned and help others, it creates a positive ripple effect in our communities.

So, as we wrap up, remember that this isn't the end. It's a moment to look back, appreciate what we've discovered, and look forward to a future filled with purpose and possibility. Frugal living isn't just a one-time thing; it's a lifelong journey of making choices that bring happiness, connection, and well-being. Let this way of life be your trusted companion, guiding you towards a tomorrow that's not just about money but about a life that's truly fulfilling.

Printed in Great Britain
by Amazon